Social Media for Veterinary Professionals

Online Community, Reputation, and Brand Management

Brenda Tassava, CVPM, CVJ

ISBN: 978-0-557-71378-3

Table of Contents

Introduction

Social media was undiscovered territory for me until my daughter Jesi began high school. At freshman registration, I was standing in line with her as two upperclass girls greeted one another excitedly at the end of the summer. As they parted, one said to the other "Facebook me later!" My daughter looked up at me for emphasis, as she had been asking permission to create a Facebook page for months.

Up until this point, MySpace had been pretty popular but seemed to be on the downswing as Facebook was gaining popularity, especially with students and young adults. Twitter was just coming on the scene and people were wondering what it was all about. Using Facebook as a business tool was unheard of, as business pages had not yet been created by the developers at Facebook.

My only motivation for creating my Facebook profile was so that I could be an informed parent. I wanted to be sure my daughter was safe, and acting appropriately online. During the exploration process, I discovered Facebook Groups. Knowing that several of my BRAC team members were active on Facebook, and we were always looking for ways to improve our internal communication, I created a Broad Ripple Animal Clinic Staff Group on Facebook and invited the entire team to join via their employee email addresses. What a can of worms I opened that day! Not only did I introduce more than half my staff to social media that day, but also I suddenly had to start questioning the benefits and drawbacks of this new resource.

I attended the VHMA Annual Conference in a few months later and during our first CVPM round table discussion, I told a group of my peers what I had done. You could have heard a pin drop in that room! The shock and disbelief was apparent by the looks on people's faces, as well as the lack of response---no one knew what to say or think! I look back at that moment with a little bit of pride now, rather than the embarrassment I felt at that moment in time. My experimentation as a parent propelled me towards becoming a social media pioneer in the veterinary profession. I was a latecomer to blogging, as many successful veterinary bloggers hit the scene well before the social media revolution, but in 2008 "social media" as it is known today hadn't crossed a lot of minds within our industry.

Before that original Group invitation was sent, approximately 10% of our team was active on Facebook. Today, that number is closer to 90%. In the spring of 2009 several cutting edge practices had already created their

4

Facebook business pages. My practice owner, Dr. David Brunner came back from a meeting and told me in no uncertain terms that I needed to start writing a blog for the clinic and "figure out this social media stuff I'm hearing about". And so, we have the second of two events that changed my path in veterinary practice management, carving out my focus in the social media world.

In the early months of social media experimentation at our practice, we underwent a lot of "trial-and-error" learning, respectable new client growth, and a complete evolution in the way we interact with our existing and potential clients, as well as with one another. I attended social media conferences outside the veterinary industry, read every book I could get my hands on, and just "tried stuff" to see what would happen. Social media is not hard. It's actually pretty easy once you find your direction and realize you are participating in a conversation, rather than creating a straight marketing or advertising strategy. I hope this book gives back "just a little" to the profession that has given so much to me. If you have feedback for me or simply want to reach out and network, I hope you'll "Facebook me"!

Brenda Tassava, CVPM, CVJ

artdogindy@facebook.com

Defining Social Media

Social media is the sharing of information, stories, photos, and experiences by individuals on the Internet, usually within online social networks. A few of these networks include:

- Facebook
- MySpace
- Twitter
- YouTube
- LinkedIn
- Flickr
- Ning
- StumbleUpon
- AOL Instant Messaging (AIM)
- Yahoo! Groups

There are literally thousands of different social networks, including custom networks that are very specific to industries, personal hobbies, and regions. For the sake of simplicity, most of this book will use examples from and refer to Facebook, as it is currently the most popular social media venue in the world (2010). The key similarity in all these different examples is that the information, or rather "medium" that is published in these venues is actually created and shared by the people participating in and connected to one another in each network. The really important thing to take notice of is that rather than "surfing the web"; people who use social media spend an incredible amount of time within these social networks. So much so that social media has overtaken pornography as the number one activity on the Internet (2009). While it's still crucial to have a great website for your veterinary practice, a kind of online brochure, it's equally important to create and maintain a presence in relevant social media networks.

Historically, individuals and small businesses have had to seek out those in the publishing industry to get their thoughts "in print". Whether it was writing a weekly column for the local paper or being asked to write an article for an industry publication, we've had little control over when and where our thoughts and beliefs have been published. As a veterinary professional, you may have written a monthly article for your neighborhood paper about pets on a frequent basis in the hopes of getting your practice's name and philosophies in front of existing and potential clients. With social media, you now have control over when and where your articles, messages and thoughts are published and they are completely searchable for an indefinite period of time. You are now in the driver's seat! This is the biggest difference between traditional media and social media: traditional media is published by others who have the power to decide when, where and if your material is published; with social media, the individual has the power to publish anything they'd like in a venue that has a lasting and reverberating impact.

Another key difference between traditional and social media is that with traditional media you are speaking to the masses in the hopes that people who are interested in what you have to say will see it. With social media, you are usually speaking directly to people with a genuine interest in what you have to say. They are a part of your social media venue because they have pets, are interested in veterinary medicine, or have heard good things about you and your practice.

The third major difference between traditional and social media is that your audience can interact and correspond directly with you. Rather than publishing a traditional piece of media, like a magazine article or book where you do all the "talking", when you publish within social media forums, your audience has the power to comment by posting their thoughts about what you've written, or even to ask questions. For this reason, it's incredibly important that you monitor your social media publications (or posts) so you can respond when necessary, and in order to actually continue the conversation. Not only is it important to respond to individuals who are commenting or asking questions, but also you must keep in mind that others are reading and following along. They are formulating opinions about you based on how you respond to social media conversations once they have begun. The more conversations you can "spark", the better. Interactivity is your gauge for how successful you are in the world of social media.

Getting Started

If social media is completely new to you, then "Congratulations!" you haven't had the opportunity to make a lot of mistakes and blunders like the rest of us who may have been early adopters. My biggest mistake would have to be inviting staff members to be friends with me on Facebook. Why is this a mistake? As the Hospital Administrator in my practice, I am in a position of authority, as are veterinarians, practice managers and team leaders. When people who hold positions of authority reach out in this manner to those they have that authority over, it makes for an awkward and sometimes tense situation. The person on the receiving end of the invitation may have many thoughts run through their head including:

- "If I ignore this invitation, will my boss hold it against me?"
- "Why does my boss want to be friends with me on Facebook when we aren't really "friendly" at work?"
- "My boss is snooping on my private life!"

You get the picture; it's just not a good idea. After this learning experience, I follow this rule, which I recommend to veterinarians, practice managers and team leaders: never friend request your staff, and if they friend request you, you must be consistent. By consistent, I mean that you should treat every staff request the same. You must decide whether or not you are going to accept these requests from your staff members ahead of time and stick to it in a consistent manner with all team members. My personal rule is that I accept all requests to be friends on Facebook by members of my staff. Your personal rule should be an "all or nothing" rule, in that you should either accept all requests or ignore all requests from staff so you are not appearing to show favoritism in any way.

Be prepared, because team members will request to become friends with you. They will do so for many reasons. Some are merely curious and may "unfriend" you within hours or days of your acceptance (once they've had a chance to read through your profile). Others may friend request you because they want to feel more involved with the clinic or be more "in the know" as to what's happening at work. Increasingly, you will find there's really no ulterior motive, as social media sites like Facebook have simply become the primary modes of communication for many of your team members and it's all about direct access and convenience.

If you are a veterinary support staff team member, then you actually sit in the driver's seat with regard to how or if you'd like to connect with your co-workers in the world of social media. You should also have your own personal rule of thumb when it comes to connecting with co-workers and peers. Are you going to connect with everyone, just your closest "work friends" or no one from work? What about clients? How will you respond to clients who request to be "friends" on Facebook? We will discuss many of these scenarios in a later chapter, but for now please consider what your personal policy might be and why. Then try to be consistent with your decision.

Whatever your professional title or job description might be, it's important to get started off on the right foot when it comes to social media. If you haven't used Facebook or Twitter, you should go ahead and create your profiles at these sites, http://www.facebook.com and http://www.twitter.com. You should fill out each field and add a personal photo at the very least. I'm not going to walk you through the step-by-step process as these sites are ever changing and being updated more frequently than most people can keep up with on a regular basis. Both sites are extremely easy to use and all you need is a valid email address to get started.

There are a few things you need to ask yourself and decide before you create your profiles. Ask yourself why you are venturing into the world of social media. Is it your hope to connect with family, friends, and clients? Are you looking for a way to increase your client base? Do you want to expand your career into other avenues such as writing or video? These are all things you should think about as you create your profiles.

With Twitter, you can be an individual or a business entity. There is no difference in the way you would go about setting up the account. Again, think about the purpose of your profile: will you be speaking to others as "Dave, the guy who loves music", as "Dr. Dave, the local veterinarian", or as "Green Acres Veterinary Hospital"? You need to decide before you create your profile, and then stick with that persona when using that profile. Alternatively, you could be all three; you just need to create a separate Twitter profile for each persona.

You should also give great consideration to your Twitter handle. A Twitter handle is @ followed by your chosen user name. Your handle should be easy to remember, and in line with your practice's overall brand or image. At Broad Ripple Animal Clinic and Wellness Center, our website address is http://www.bracpet.com and so we are @BRACpet on Twitter and our Facebook page can be found at http://www.facebook.com/BRACpet. This shortened acronym

14

(BRACpet) made sense to us because of our original website address. Now, not only clients, but also other small businesses in our local community, as well as those in the global veterinary community recognize @BRACpet.

My primary Twitter profiles are @bktassava and @BRACpet. I also help manage several other accounts, in cooperation with a few colleagues. However, I am solely responsible for the tweets from @bktassava and @BRACpet. As @bktassava, I am a "wife, mother, certified veterinary practice manager who loves creating art." This is my profile description word-for-word and describes who I am and what I represent when I am tweeting as @bktassava. Notice that I combined aspects of my personal life and my professional life to not only give me more flexibility in my tweets, but to also allow myself to be *myself*, or rather to display my true personality. As a veterinary professional, I try to conduct myself in a professional manner when discussing topics relative to practice management, team building, and other veterinary workplace topics. It's incredibly important to pair this professionalism with shades of your true personality for a more dynamic online profile, or persona in the social media world. After all, outside of the online world you are not fully defined by your career, and neither should your career fully determine your online personality. Your primary goal should be to connect with and meet new people in the social media forum, which will hopefully translate to new relationships in real life.

My second Twitter profile as @BRACpet is described as an "innovative, progressive veterinary practice in Indianapolis." When I represent @BRACpet online, I am representing the entire practice along with our core values and philosophies. With each and every post or comment, I must represent the Broad Ripple Animal Clinic and Wellness Center, and NOT my personal self. This is the most important thing to remember if you are managing social media for your practice or an organization. Never insert your personal beliefs and feelings into your posts. Always stop and ask yourself, "Does this post reflect the core values and philosophy of our practice?" before you publish your comments.

Giving your veterinary practice a Facebook presence first requires you to have a personal profile. It's very important to set both up properly to avoid issues down the road. First, register as a person, setting up your personal profile. Again, think through the information you post for others to read. Ask yourself, "Am I posting information I would share with a client or co-worker?" If you can't answer "yes", then it's probably not appropriate to share at all. You need to keep in mind that once you are on Facebook, or any other social media platform where clients co-exist, they WILL seek you out, and you need to be prepared for it. Look at social media as a way to extend yourself into the community even further. Instead of running into a client at the grocery store or a restaurant, look at Facebook as an opportunity to "run into" any number of clients at any time of day. They will get to know your personal side, especially if you also use social media to stay in touch with friends and family. And what's the harm in being a "real person" to your clients, as long as everything is appropriate and socially acceptable?

There's a term that is frequently used in the social media world, and that word is *transparency*. The very nature of social media requires that you be as transparent as possible. In other words, don't pretend to be something or somebody that you are not. Avoid hiding behind your logo, and be a very real person while maintaining a professional image on behalf of your practice. Transparency also refers to the way in which you respond to client concerns in a social media venue. You need to avoid that knee-jerk reaction of deleting comments that you just don't like. Always remember that the way in which you handle negative (and positive) comments can and will be viewed by many, many others to read. Be true to yourself, humble in your apologies, and ever responsive to your community. This is social media transparency.

You need to spend some time using Facebook on a personal level before attempting to manage a business profile for your practice. You will need to get used to common social media etiquette and spend several weeks, if not months simply observing, listening, and conversing on a personal level before taking it to the next level. Search out other veterinary practices and "like" these pages in order to stream them into your newsfeed. Search for your local animal shelters, the American Animal Hospital Association, the American Veterinary Medical Associations and even your state's veterinary medical association. You will find most, if not all to already have a presence on Facebook. Search for friends and family members and build your list of Facebook friends, interacting with people with whom you already have relationships before striking them up with existing and potential clients. The more you "practice" social media, the better you will become at communicating in this venue.

Once you have a personal profile and have spent a few weeks on Facebook, you should create your practice's page by creating a "business page", not another personal profile. If you do this correctly, people will be able to "like" your page rather than "add as a friend". You will be the administrator of the business page, and when you post to your practice's wall, your practice's photo will display as the avatar, and NOT your personal photo. As with any social media profile, please fill-in all information fields as completely as possible and add a photo of your building or your practice's logo as the profile photo. While photos of your entire staff might look nice on the wall in a big frame, they do not do your practice justice when displayed as a Facebook profile photo. Avoid using images that are too crowded or when made tiny, lose their representational nature.

You and your practice now have social media presences! A presence is very different from a strategy and should not be confused with one another. We have merely gotten you started with setting up profiles and discussing some things you need to consider when building these profiles. In the next few chapters, we will explore creating a social media strategy, creating a social media policy, training for your team, as well as scheduling and management tactics for your social media platform.

Veterinary Blogging

Before you can create or plan your social media strategy, you should have a practice blog. There are many reasons for blogging, but if you are looking for a way to communicate with your clients and draw traffic to your practice's website, then a blog is the most effective tool you have available to your practice. Not only is it cost-effective (FREE), but it has the power to propel your website to the top of online searches. A blog is technically an online journal or log (Web + Log = Blog).

Think of your website and your blog as having two separate functions. Your website should be created as your "online practice brochure". With that in mind, there should be great thought given to the design, the exact wording and descriptions you'd like to use, the staff biographies and photos, etc. All of these elements should remain fairly static. Your blog is quite different. A blog is designed to generate new information on a frequent basis. This information can be in the form of educational handouts, newsletter articles, or simply conversations with your readers. Your blog should be updated frequently and consistently for maximum effectiveness. When your website and blog are interconnected online, your blog draws people to your website through search engines. Search engines love new content, so the more robust your blog, the more traffic you will see to your website and hopefully through your practice's door.

There are many blog platforms available to you, and most of them are free to use. Rather than recommend one over another, my best advice is to work with your web designer to find a blog platform they are familiar with, so it can be attached directly to your existing practice website. I have the most experience with Wordpress, simply because I met a lot of IT professionals in my area who use Wordpress, which made it easy to learn and integrate with our practice's website. Our web designer added our practice's blog to Broad Ripple Animal Clinic and Wellness Center's website (http://bracpet.com) by making it a part of the website at http://bracpet.com/blog for maximum online traffic.

Not sure what to write about? Start with all those handouts you've been meaning to update. You know, the ones you wrote 10 or 15 years ago that you continue to hand to clients when their pet is in for a specific medical problem. Start by editing these handouts, adding new pictures and current information, and then instead of making a bunch of copies and putting them in a hanging file folder, publish them to your blog and send clients directly to your site to read! Not only are you becoming more environmentally friendly, but you are generating traffic to your website and teaching your clients that YOU are their online veterinary resource for information about their pets.

No matter which blogging platform you choose, it should supply you with the tools you need to monitor and measure your success. Site statistics that show you how many people visit your blog each day, along with the keyword searches used to find your blog are a must. With this information, you'll be able to see what posts people are most interested in and create new posts based on this vital information.

A few more pieces of advice to keep in mind when blogging:

- Keep your posts brief and to the point. Anything more than 400-600 words and you'll lose your reader's attention span in most cases.

- Make your posts personal by telling a story. There's nothing more compelling than incorporating a real-life success story when explaining a course of therapy for a pet's disease. Just remember to respect your patient and client confidentiality by not revealing names, and seeking permission to use images in photos.

- Use photo images within each post whenever possible. Take it a step further by video-blogging on occasion or creating your own

YouTube channel for videos, which can be linked to within a blog post.

- If you truly struggle with writing, or simply don't have the time, you can subscribe to a service such as Veterinary News Network. For an annual subscription fee, you will have access to professionally written blog stories, videos and articles, which you can customize to fit your practice and then publish to your own blog, website, or newsletter.

Before you proceed any further with a social media strategy, you should have a blog, either as a veterinary professional or on behalf of your practice, as well as a practice website. You should also now have a Twitter and Facebook profile, along with a business page for your veterinary practice and possibly (advisably) a Twitter profile for your practice. Let's move on to your social media strategy.

Social Media Strategy for Your Veterinary Practice's Success

Before you wander down the social media path, you need to determine why you are embarking on this trip. New technologies and communication tools are great, but unless you have a plan in place you could just end up wasting your valuable time. Ask yourself what you hope to accomplish with social media, personally and professionally.

- Do you want to increase your practice's number of new clients?

- Do you want to better bond with your existing clients?

- Are you looking for a way to maximize efficiency relative to your client communications?

- Do you want your practice to become more environmentally friendly?

- Do you want to brand your practice as THE place to take pets for veterinary care in your community?

- Do you want to make yourself known as the "friendly, neighborhood veterinarian" who responds to pet care questions anytime, anyplace?

- Do you want to promote new products and services to your clients?

- Are you looking for ways to better communicate internally, with your team?

- Is your practice poised for growth in a demographic area that supports advanced technologies?

- Do you want to build rapport and network with other veterinary professionals on a more personal level?

- Is client education important to you and your team?

Decide exactly what you hope to accomplish using social media. Once you have determined your goal, you can then build a strategy for achieving it. I highly recommend you use a SMART goal-setting method in order to construct your strategy, whatever the end goal might be for you and your practice.

Look at each goal and evaluate it. For example, many practices express a desire to increase the number of new clients they see each month. What steps will you need to take to reach your goal? Are you being specific enough about your goal?

- S = Specific
- M = Measurable

- A = Attainable

- R = Realistic

- T = Timely

By setting a specific goal, it will help you focus on your efforts and clearly define what it is you are going to do. When setting a Specific goal, think about the following:

- WHAT are you going to do?

- WHY is it important to do at this time?

- HOW are you going to do it?

Setting a measurable goal allows you to manage it. Examples of measurable goals include:

- Increase the number of new clients seen by 10

- Increase the number of new clients seen by 15%

- Increase appointment fill rate to ≥ 2 per hour

Attainable and realistic are inter-related. You need to set goals that are realistic for your practice, and that you can envision yourself achieving if you make some changes to what you are currently doing. Don't set yourself up for failure by setting "pie-in-the-sky" goals!

Set-up time parameters for your goals, whether it be monthly, quarterly or even annually. You may be working towards setting monthly goals, based on what your previous month looks like. Avoid time parameters that are open-ended or too far in the future to really track and make adjustments as needed.

Most veterinary professionals I work with have social media goals that revolve around attracting new clients, bonding with existing clients, and building an online reputation that is attractive to peers, as well as potential and existing clients. For that reason, we are going to break down these goals and outline specific strategies in the next three chapters.

Branding Yourself: Online Reputation Management

When was the last time you Googled yourself? You know: entered your first and last name into Google's (or Bing's, or Yahoo's, etc.) search engine to see what results you get back. If you haven't ever done this, or it's been a while, you need to start doing it on a consistent, regular basis. If you think your clients aren't doing it, you would be wrong! This is the important first step in managing your online brand, or reputation. You should be doing this for yourself, as a veterinary professional, as well as your practice.

Go ahead and Google yourself! What did your search yield? Is the information relevant to "you" or someone else who happens to have the same or similar name? If you Googled your practice's name, did your website or blog come up first? If it didn't, then you need to takes steps to change this for your practice and yourself.

I need to remind you that I am a mom and a veterinary practice manager, which are the two things that landed me in the middle of social media. I am NOT an experienced Information Technologies person, a Search Engine Optimization expert, nor do I have a deep understanding of software development. Everything I know and share with you is based on experience and what I have learned from others who are experts in these areas. I will convey everything I have learned in simplified layman's terminology, so if you have experience in these areas, please do not begrudge me for simplifying things too much for your level of expertise. My goal is to help veterinary professionals incorporate social media into their professional lives, no matter their level of experience or understanding.

In working with young and experienced veterinarians for the past several years, I have found they have little to no awareness of their online reputation. Most have never Googled their own name. I believe it is a very important thing to do, at least once a month. You can take some very simple steps to have better control over the information that comes up in these searches, which impacts what clients, peers, and friends find about you on the Internet.

The first thing you should do, whether you are a veterinarian, a practice manager, or any other level of veterinary professional is create a profile for yourself on LinkedIn (http://www.linkedin.com). This social media site has tremendous search power and if you have an existing LinkedIn profile, it should come up on the first page of an online search for your name. As with any social media profile, you need to complete your profile in its entirety, along with a professional photo of yourself. You should think of LinkedIn as a sort of reception or social gathering of your colleagues and business acquaintances. Your LinkedIn profile asks for details of your education and work experience, as well as gives you the opportunity to list awards and professional recognitions. If you have any areas of special interest or expertise, list them on your LinkedIn profile. Once you begin networking with others in the veterinary profession within this social media platform, you will meet people who might seek you out for your specialized knowledge and expertise.

Best practices for LinkedIn include limiting your status updates and comments to those that have to do with what is going on in your professional life. This is the one venue I highly recommend you keep strictly professional. Don't talk about what you had for dinner or the most recent movie you watched. This platform is designed to be a professional social media venue. Status updates should reflect what you are doing in your career, whether it is learning an advanced surgical procedure, attending a continuing education conference, or reading a business book.

You can choose to automatically post your LinkedIn status updates to your Twitter account. This is common practice and drives followers on Twitter to your LinkedIn profile, where they can learn more about you as a veterinary professional and connect or network with you on LinkedIn.

There are many veterinary specific groups on LinkedIn that you can join, based on your professional interests. As a member of these LinkedIn groups, you will have the opportunity to join in discussions relevant to the veterinary profession. You will also meet, or connect with other veterinary professionals when you join these groups. Take some time to explore LinkedIn, finding colleagues you already know in person, and meeting those who share common interests.

Once you have joined the LinkedIn network, be sure to frequent it on a regular basis, so your profile does not become stagnant. Any time you have a career change such as a new certification, a newly published article or book, or even a new job title, it would be in your best interest to update your profile by posting this information. If you move or change employers, this is the first place you should go and update your current information online. Otherwise, your former employer's information will continue to come up when your name is searched online.

A LinkedIn profile not only helps you, the veterinary professional, manage your online reputation, but it also helps your practice's online brand awareness. By completing your profile, and listing your practice's name as your current place of business, you have paired your practice's name with LinkedIn for that valuable search power. If every Associate in your practice does the same, your practice's name will rise in terms of search engine ranking.

Your blog posts can also enhance online reputation management. If you are a veterinarian and you write posts for your practice's blog, along with others, be sure your posts list your full name in the byline. Search engines love blogs because they are updated frequently with new information, and so the posts you write will appear whenever your name is entered in an online search engine. The more control you have over what appears when your name is Googled, the better.

In addition to performing a monthly scheduled Google search of your name and your practice's name, you should also use a few Internet monitoring tools that will assist you in learning when new information is posted online. Google Alerts is the most valuable of these monitoring tools. When activated, you will receive email alerts whenever new information is found online that mention whatever keywords or phrases you request. I highly recommend you set-up Google Alerts for your full name, your practice's name, and the full names of each one of the Associates in your practice. Whatever new information appears on the Internet, whether it's good or bad, you'll know about it within 24 hours. There is nothing worse than a bad online review floating around out there that you have no knowledge of, or opportunity to respond to before hundreds or even thousands of people read it.

Now that we're on the topic, how do you handle a negative review or comment that you find about either yourself or your practice? The manner in which you respond is ultimately up to you, but there are several things to consider. When you read a negative review or online comment, don't respond immediately. Take some time to read through it a few times before investigating the circumstances that led to your client's frustration.

Everyone fears the horrible online review posted by a disgruntled employee under a pseudonym, but the truth of the matter is that this rarely happens. If it does happen, you can take steps to pursue the removal of a fraudulent post by gathering your facts and pursuing it with the site where it appears. It might take some time, but thorough documentation will go a long way.

The more likely scenario is one where a client is frustrated and feels he or she has exhausted all avenues for resolution with you or your practice. You might not even be aware of the situation until you read about it online, because perhaps the source of the frustration was an encounter with a team member, or lack of follow-up by the office manager. Most people don't go out of their way to post a negative comment or review unless they have attempted to correct the situation and feel they have been ignored or treated unfairly. It is extremely important that you not react before you do as much research into the matter as you can, in terms of reviewing the client and patient records. You should then show the review to the staff members who were involved during the client's last visit to gain their insight into why this particular client might be unhappy. Then it is time to pick up the phone and call this client to open up a discussion.

Don't just leave a voice mail message and wait for the client to return your call; pursue this client until you get a chance to speak one-on-one. Let the client know that their happiness is important to you and you'd like to do whatever it takes to resolve any lingering frustration they might be feeling. Then, sit back and listen. Listen with an open mind and listen with the idea that "perception is reality" as your point of reference. You might not agree with or like what the client has to say, but their perception of the incident is the only thing that truly matters. Then, do what you can to repair the relationship with this particular client. Apologize, if an apology is warranted. Go back to your staff and provide them with the insight and training they need in order to avoid these repercussions in the future, through prevention. If you can prevent a client from reaching this level of frustration, then you shouldn't see negative reviews or comments in the future because you will have worked with them to resolve their concerns before they ever escalate to this point. In many cases, once you have opened up the lines of communication and worked out the client's concern, the client will usually modify or retract their negative review or comments as an act of good faith. If they don't do this after a few weeks, call them again and ask them if they wouldn't mind modifying or updating their online comments. In all likelihood, if the relationship has been repaired, your client will be happy to accommodate your request.

An alternative to this scenario is one where you reach out to the client and they are either nonresponsive or unreasonable in their complaints or demands. You must decide for yourself at what point you cannot move forward in trying to mend the relationship. If you have made an effort to address the client's concerns in a reasonable manner, and are unable to make progress, then you may decide to address their negative remarks openly within the context of the original online complaint. Extreme caution should be taken, though for if not worded exactly right could fan the flames unnecessarily, and may appear to be defensive on your part. A wiser approach would be to ignore the comment once you've tried to address your client's concerns. Then, approach several clients who are happy with your services asking them to post their own reviews to the same site. This will effectively bury the negative comment with several positive comments, giving online readers a more balanced review of your veterinary services.

There is nothing wrong with asking for online reviews from your very best clients. Just be sure your clients are the ones doing the actual reviews and not staff or family members. Due to the nature of the Internet, a positive review that appears to be "planted" is worse than an authentic negative review, since this brings your integrity into question.

You now have a branding strategy for yourself and your practice. Managed effectively, you will be able to build a positive, dynamic online reputation using LinkedIn, your practice's blog, and monitoring your online mentions. Used in conjunction with other social media platforms like Facebook and Twitter, you will be able to quickly build a rich online brand that is attractive to potential and existing clients and colleagues.

Social Media Strategy: Bonding With Your Clients

Veterinary medicine is about much more than patient care; it's also about the relationships we form that sometimes last a lifetime. As veterinary professionals, we have an obligation to act as advocates for our patients, who cannot speak for themselves. This requires us to communicate with and form relationships with the people who are bonded to our patients; they are our clients. The stronger the relationship between us and our clients, the better care we'll be able to provide to our patients.

For this reason, bonding with our clients deserves a great deal of on-going attention. Historically, we have done this by calling clients with diagnostic results, sending patient reminder postcards, and publishing monthly or quarterly newsletters. Social media takes these concepts to a completely different level. We now have the opportunity to not only bond more directly with our clients one-on-one, but to also build communities of clients who are enthusiastic about their pets and the services we provide. Within these communities, our clients can even choose to bond with one another, sharing stories and photos of their own pets. This kind of bonding enhances individual confidences in our veterinary care. After all, there's strength in numbers and when clients are able to mingle with one another and express confidence and satisfaction with your care, then your stock rises in everyone's minds.

Bonding with our existing clients through the use of social media is a strategy that employs several tools. A basic toolkit will consist of:

- An e-newsletter: either privately hosted with a company such as Constant Contact, or through a veterinary-specific provider like VetStreet.

- Twitter profiles and accounts for your practice and/or your veterinarians.

- A practice blog that is an integral part of your practice's main website.

- A Facebook page for your practice.

- An online pet portal account for your clients integrated with your practice management software.

- A YouTube channel for your practice, http://www.youtube.com.

You may think to yourself, "Most of my clients don't use email". This may have been true ten years ago, but times and communication technologies have changed dramatically. Not only do most people have an email address, which they use at least once a day, but also more and more people are using their phones to access the Internet, rather than the traditional desktop computer. At this very moment, I am sitting in a remote cabin in northern Michigan with no Internet access, yet I am updating Broad Ripple Animal Clinic and Wellness Center's Facebook page with our holiday weekend hours, using the Facebook application on my mobile phone. This means, we can connect with our clients virtually anytime, anywhere with the tools in our social media toolkit.

With an email address, you are able to strengthen the bond between your clients and your practice through a pet portal, where they can request appointments, view their pets' reminders, order medication refills, upload their pets' photos, and more. This is a vital part of your bonding strategy. Clients who can connect with you, on their own terms and at their convenience are much more likely to remain loyal, lifelong clients.

E-Newsletters

The other tool where an email address is vital is your e-newsletter. Whether monthly or quarterly, it's time to "go green" and convert those printed, hard copy newsletters to an electronic version that arrives in your client's email inbox on a regular basis. You will not only save money, but it is also more environmentally friendly. There are a variety of e-newsletter service providers available to you for a reasonable cost. They all function in much the same way, providing you with newsletter templates that are attractive and easy to use. If you have a practice blog, then you already have material for your newsletter. There's no need to write for both your blog and a newsletter, since you can use your e-newsletter to drive your clients to your blog, which drives them to your website, and opens the door for questions and direct communication with the practice. If you take three or four blog posts and insert the first few sentences of each post into a separate section of your newsletter, along with a link to the post on your blog, with a description "click here for full story", you will drive traffic to your blog. You will also be able to view which stories generated the most interest by reviewing the reports section for each edition of your e-newsletter. This is extremely valuable information, as you can generate more blog posts around the articles your clients are most interested in reading. With this approach, if you are writing a new blog post each week, then you will easily be able to put together a monthly e-newsletter, using your weekly blog posts in a matter of one hour each month.

Twitter

Using Twitter to bond with current clients might not seem to be as much of a return on your investment in time and energy, but you'll be surprised at the depth of bonding you will see when you use this platform. Veterinary professionals should use Twitter for five activities:

- To have conversations with existing and potential clients.
- To have conversations with other veterinary professionals.
- To network with other local businesses that use Twitter.
- To monitor breaking news stories that might be of interest to you and your clients.
- And to drive people to new blog posts and pet care links of interest.

If you're not doing one of these five things, then you are probably wasting your time on Twitter. For this particular chapter, let's focus strictly on conversations with clients, breaking news, and driving people to new blog posts.

You've joined Twitter and completed your profile, now what? Check out the resources at the back of this book. I have listed several Twitter handles of veterinary professionals from around the country who are active on Twitter. I would begin by "following" each one of these colleagues. When you "follow" someone, it brings their "tweets" into your Twitter feed, which is filtered by your selections. When you "follow" someone, they receive a notification that you have started following them, along with a brief description of who you are, based on the profile you completed. If your profile appeals to them, they may choose to "follow" you, pulling your tweets into their feed. This begins the conversation between you and others on Twitter.

To start following clients or to let clients know you are on Twitter, you can do several things. You can post a badge or announcement on your website's home page, letting everyone know you are on Twitter. You can let clients know by posting a message at the bottom of your invoices, telling them how to find you on Twitter. You can also use your marquee sign to let your community know how to find you on Twitter. You should also include your Twitter handle (@ followed by your Twitter name) in your email signature, so clients and colleagues will find you more readily.

You should also do frequent searches on Twitter to see if your practice is being mentioned. You might be surprised to see that clients are already posting comments and even photos to Twitter, unaware that you are now a part of the platform. When you see these mentions, choose to "follow" the people who are talking about you. This will open up the line of communication between you and your clients.

Whenever I find a client who is on Twitter, I make a note in their chart, listing their Twitter handle. This alerts the staff whenever they see or interact with the client that they are active on social media platforms. What can your team do with this information? If a client has admitted their patient for surgery, your team can take photos of their pet resting post-operatively and Tweet the photo directly to the client that all is well. If a client is active on Twitter, odds are they also participate in other social media platforms like Facebook, and are technologically savvy. These clients might prefer email communications to telephone communications. You can customize your communications approach to your clients on an individual basis, simply by making notes of their preferences.

If you correspond with clients using email communications, it's a simple task to copy and paste these conversations and include them in your electronic medical records. This is much more efficient and accurate than writing a synopsis of each conversation you have with a client. You can also copy and paste lab results directly into your outgoing email communications, which many clients deeply appreciate.

Most people who use Twitter use it as a "newsfeed". They scan their feed periodically throughout the day to see if there's any breaking news in their community, or a new story that interests them. You can pass along pertinent pet care stories by finding them in your Twitter feed and "Re-Tweeting" (RT in front of the post means someone has Re-Tweeted a particular Tweet) so that your followers can also benefit from the information. As a veterinary professional, your followers will view your Tweets and Re-Tweets to be "sourced", so be sure to thoroughly read anything you Re-Tweet, especially if it contains a link to a blog post or news article.

Twitter is an excellent place to alert people that you have just written and published a new blog post. The best approach is to announce the story with a brief description to spark interest, followed by a link to the blog post. There is a 140-character limit for all Tweets, so you may find yourself using a url shortener like bitly.com or Hootsuite's built-in url shortener (http://www.hootsuite.com) to keep your Tweets from being too long to post with a link. When used in this manner, Twitter is another tool you can use to drive readers to your blog, which drives them to your website, and hopefully through your practice's door more frequently.

46

Facebook

If Facebook were a country (2010), it would be the third largest country in the world, behind China and India. Will Facebook be as predominant a force ten years from now? It's hard to tell, and more than likely the next great thing will have taken its place. For now, Facebook is a major player and your practice needs to have a presence.

As I mentioned before, I'm not going to walk you through setting up your practice's Facebook page, as things change on a fairly frequent basis and by the time this book is published, the steps for set-up may very well be outdated. Set-up is a fairly straightforward step-by-step process that most anyone can accomplish. The most important thing is to make sure you are creating a business page for your practice, and NOT a personal page. How do you know if you've done it right? If there's a button that says "like this page" at the top of your Facebook page, then you've set it up properly. However, if the button reads, "add as a friend", then you will need to delete the page and start again. It is extremely important that you not try to use a personal page as your practice's business page. If reported to or discovered by Facebook, your page will be taken down and Facebook will permanently ban your email address. If you are considering hiring a person experienced in social media to manage your practice's social media strategy, set-up of your profiles and pages is the only area I can see where a hired person's experience will be beneficial to you. It should take them a few short hours to get everything up and running for you or an experienced staff member to take over and manage.

The reason I don't recommend you hire an outside "social media expert" to manage your practice's strategy is that your clients will quickly become savvy to what is going on. The very nature of social media is that it is a social experience whereby people connect and network with one another. A hired consultant does not know your practice, your philosophy, or even veterinary medicine. When clients choose to interact with you within a social media platform, they choose to do so because they believe they are interacting with YOU or your staff, not a paid outsider. They are choosing to build a closer relationship with your practice. If they discover the relationship they have built is with a paid stranger who is a marketing guru, then you will have damaged the relationship you sought to make stronger. This is where transparency comes in to play. You must be transparent in everything you do within the world of social media, or your followers will lose trust in you. Don't put yourself out there as something you are not. If "Dr. Dave" is the person clients think they are interacting with on Facebook, then it had better be "Dr. Dave" doing all the posts and updates and comments himself. When I follow Dr. Marty Becker on Facebook, I expect his posts and comments to come directly from him, and they do. When I comment back, I feel as if I am speaking directly to him. Whenever he is unable to comment, and his colleague Gina posts for him in his absence, she lets followers know it is she and not Dr. Becker. This is what transparency is all about, and it is vital to the success of your social media efforts.

The thing that is truly different about Facebook when compared to earlier hyped websites and online networks is that people who use Facebook tend to stay on Facebook for long periods of time, rather than surfing the Internet. Facebook has found a way to bring everything a person is interested in to one place: the individual Facebook newsfeed.

The Facebook newsfeed is your practice's opportunity to create conversations and interact with your clients in a forum where their friends can also see these conversations. Once a client "likes" your page, don't expect them to visit your page frequently. Most people actually never visit a business page again after "liking" it. All the interactions take place in their newsfeed. For this reason, it's vitally important that you post to your wall at least once or twice a day, most days of the week. You need to find the times of day that generate the most reaction, by way of comments and "likes" to your posts. If you post every morning at 7:00am so you can get it out of the way, and you aren't getting very many comments or new followers, chances are your posts are getting buried in your clients' newsfeeds and are going unnoticed.

While number of followers is important, your true return on investment can be seen in your weekly Facebook reports. The more "active" your followers, and the more "likes" and "comments" you get to your posts each week, the more effective your social media efforts are for your practice. Your goal should be to create a variety of posts that cause your followers to want to interact with you and other followers.

- Ask questions! This approach usually sparks great conversations with many clients in a single post.
- Post cute or funny pet photos you capture throughout the day. People have a genuine interest in what we do and love seeing photos of puppies, kittens, dogs and cats. You should avoid the use of photos that you might view as "cool" because it's unusual, like a dog vs. porcupine photograph. These photos are not the "warm and fuzzy" ones that clients love to see!
- Post links to your newest blog posts (again, driving clients to your blog, which drives them to your website, and hopefully through the practice's door more frequently).

- Post photos of staff members wishing them a happy birthday, or happy anniversary when they reach milestones with your practice.

- Let clients know when a doctor or staff member has attended a conference and brought back new techniques and reached new levels of expertise.

- Post links to videos on your practice's YouTube channel.

- Post digital x-rays or digital photographs of interesting x-rays, and ask clients to guess what they might be viewing (this is a great post when you have x-rays of ingested foreign objects).

The more variety your posts have, the better. Mix things up; use lots of images and your Facebook community of pet lovers will grow.

YouTube

I mentioned YouTube, and linking to it from your Facebook page. Did you know that the #2 search engine in the world in 2010 was YouTube (#1 was Google)? People are moving more and more away from the written word and towards video because it's quicker to watch a video than to read an article. Your practice should have a YouTube account, along with your practice's own branded channel where clients can subscribe and easily find all your videos. Today's technology makes video so much easier for anyone to do. All you really need is a digital camera that takes video or a small handheld digital video camera. Some of these devices have been designed to upload video directly to YouTube in one simple step, and the investment is usually less than $200. I carry my iPhone with me everywhere. With it, and other smartphone devices, you can take photos and videos, and using a Facebook application, upload your content directly from your phone in a matter of seconds. Your videos can capture a c-section, introduce new clients to the practice with a virtual tour, or demonstrate proper pet care with short "how to" videos.

Does all this "client bonding" sound like a fulltime job in and of itself? Managing your social media strategy is really not as cumbersome as it might appear at first glance. With a little practice, and some basic organization and planning, you will find it can effectively be done in a few hours each week. The area you want to be sure not to overlook is monitoring your social media platforms. Everyday, you should take a few minutes to scan your newsfeeds on all your platforms. Perform a few quick searches for keywords relevant to you and your practice. Then be sure to use these "mentions" as a conversation-starter, responding directly to the person who made the original comment. Never fall into the habit of simply broadcasting your material without stopping to listen to what others are saying, and then responding. NO ONE is that interesting, and your followers will quickly turn you off, if they feel you aren't listening

and responding to them.

Social Media Strategy: Attracting New Clients

Attrition is a natural part of any business. In the veterinary profession, we must work at attracting new clients in order to offset attrition and maintain growth. With your new client bonding strategy, you will hopefully reduce some of your attrition by creating stronger relationships with your existing clients. Attracting new clients is another common social media strategy that can be carried out simultaneously with other strategies.

The value of traditional advertising has declined in recent years. Consumers have become very skeptical of paid advertising campaigns, and unless found to be highly entertaining are completely ignored. We have reached the point where consumers have been so flooded with mass media that they are able to tune out the messages that advertising and traditional marketing try to send. Technology has enabled consumers to skip over television advertisements with DVR, eliminate radio advertisements through Satellite radio, and bypass daily newspapers by getting their news delivered online.

From a consumer standpoint, social media is the equivalent of word-of-mouth recommendations on steroids. There is nothing more powerful than the opinion of another consumer who has had a personal experience with a service provider. Their opinion, published online in a social media venue for thousands of people to see is worth exponentially more than a paid advertisement. The best thing about social media is that as long as we (veterinary professionals) are doing a really good job, then we don't even have to ask for these recommendations---they just happen! And when they happen again and again, your practice's name is suddenly familiar to those in your community and new clients will pick up the phone and call you.

When you utilize the tools described in the previous chapter, and your clients are engaged with you in the world of social media, you will automatically "turn on" your new client strategy. Imagine that you have 1,000 clients following you on Facebook and Twitter. If each of those 1,000 clients has 100 friends they interact with regularly online, then every time they mention you by name, or post a comment to your wall, or Tweet a photo of their pets at your office, then potentially 10,000 people will see this in their newsfeeds in one way or another. This is the power of viral messages. Not every message will be seen, but the more often your practice's name is mentioned in a positive manner, the more times it is seen and over time clients will come through your practice's door. Let's look at a few examples of how this might work for your practice.

Team Influence

One of the best ways to get your social media subscriber base up and going is to encourage your staff members to subscribe themselves. In turn, they can then recommend to their social media friends and family that they "like" or "follow" your practice on Facebook and Twitter. Hopefully, this wave will continue with true fans continuing to recommend you to their friends and family online, and in person. This is known as a ripple effect, and the more passionate your team is, the more powerful this effect can be for your practice.

Sharing Posts and Re-Tweeting

Whenever you generate strong, compelling or extremely interesting content and you post it, your ultimate hope is that others will find it valuable enough to share with those in their network of friends and family. On Twitter, this is called a "Re-Tweet" and is abbreviated by "RT" at the beginning of these Tweets that re-post your original information.

Re-Tweets are a return on your investment of time and energy because they validate you as an interesting, credible source of information. By posting a RT, someone is validating and endorsing what you have to say. This again creates the ripple effect within their own circle of friends and followers, who will hopefully discover YOU when they find value in the post, as well.

On Facebook, your followers can "share" a post or link they like from your wall. This effectively introduces your practice's Facebook page to the newsfeeds of their friends. If they like what they see, they can also choose to "like" your page, pulling your posts into your newsfeed. Over time, these potential clients will become acquainted with you before they ever set foot through the doors of your practice.

Partnering With Humane Societies and Animal Welfare Groups

You may already partner with your local humane society and other shelter groups by providing veterinary services at a reduced cost, or offering health screenings to newly adopted pets. You can use social media in a similar manner, positioning yourself as a partner in a different way. Your local Humane Society probably has a social media presence. One approach that is mutually beneficial is to have a "virtual food drive" for your local shelter. In many cases, you may be able to acquire pet food from your distributor if you are willing to advertise their participation, as well. Let your followers know that for every new "like" to your Facebook page, you will donate a can (or pound) of pet food to your local shelter. The shelter can cross-post this information, directing their followers to your practice's page, exposing you to a new audience of social media participants. This works really well especially around the holidays, or a specific event. You will need to set a timeframe for your food drive and continue to post reminders each day, encouraging your followers to ask their friends to "like" you.

During the Thanksgiving and Christmas holiday weeks of 2010, Broad Ripple Animal Clinic and Wellness Center partnered with Royal Canin to raise and donate 960 cans of dog food to the Humane Society of Indianapolis with two similar campaigns. By gaining new followers and encouraging existing followers to "check-in" at Broad Ripple Animal Clinic and Wellness Center on Facebook places, the campaign raised overall awareness of the practice and the Humane Society within the Indianapolis community. While a direct correlation cannot be determined, new client numbers for the months of November and December of 2010 were up 24% from the same months the previous year. Keep in mind this Facebook page is a rather mature page, having been in existence for more than 18 months and having more than 1,400 followers at the time of the food drives, so it generated more activity than a younger page might.

Another social media partnership possibility would be the cross posting of adoptable animals. Your practice could help your local shelter or humane society by featuring an adoptable "pet-of-the-week" with a photo and the pet's story. By extending your local shelter's reach into the community, you are helping homeless pets find homes and demonstrating your natural drive to give back to the community. As time goes by, we'll probably see many new and creative ways to maximize social media for mutually beneficial outcomes.

Local Networking

Small businesses everywhere have embraced the power of social media. We are seeing more and more new businesses get off the ground and become quite successful with a marketing strategy that is purely social. When small businesses in local communities become social together, they can maximize the feeling of community, in an online forum that can and will translate to the real world.

When you follow other local businesses, they will more than likely reciprocate, which opens the door for conversations between local business owners and their patrons. Look for local restaurants, coffee shops, local news anchors and weather personalities on Twitter and Facebook. When they follow you in return, you will hopefully become their "go-to" expert for pet care questions, and their default when discussing pets with their customers and consumers. All of these opportunities lead to increased new client potential for your practice.

Social Media Management

You've created all your profiles, set-up accounts and pages, and developed your social media strategy. Now how do you manage it all without pulling you away from your main focus of caring for people and their pets?

Your first impulse might be to hire someone with social media experience to manage it for you. Personally, I don't believe this is the route to go. People who participate in social media expect to interact with YOU, not a paid social media guru. This doesn't mean the practice owner is the only person who should be managing the social media platforms for your practice! Your Social Media Manager should be someone who is deeply entrenched in the core values and philosophies of your practice, and has a total understanding of your practice's marketing philosophies and standards. More than likely this will be your Hospital Administrator, Practice Manager, or Office Manager. Large practices (more than six fulltime equivalent veterinarians) may choose to hire a dedicated, fulltime Social Media Manager. In these cases, look for someone with a great deal of social media experience, who has a marketing or journalism background. Once hired, you should spend several weeks training them to fully understand your practice, setting aside time for them to personally get to know the doctors and staff. Remember, this person must be able to speak as the "voice of your practice" in their role as your Social Media Manager. You might consider someone who works from home part of the week, but at least half the week should be done from the practice. They will need this time to take photographs, create videos, talk to staff, and be a part of practice. If they work solely from home, they'll quickly lose the pulse of the practice and their material will not be authentic.

Hospital Administrators and Managers already have a lot on their plates, so adding social media management to their "to-do" list might seem daunting. There is a learning and practice curve that can monopolize a great deal of your time in the beginning. Once you have things up and running and are comfortable with the flow, there are several steps you can take to minimize the amount of time you dedicate to this daily task.

- Managers develop strategic plans each year for their practices, and the same should be done for your practice's social media plan. Use a monthly planner to outline pet-related topics that can be incorporated into your social media posts. This can be broken down into weekly topics, based on the main topic chosen for each month.

- Set aside time to read each week. You should give yourself two to three hours each week to go through industry publications, read other blogs, and pet-specific articles. Subscribe to magazines whose target audience is pet-lovers. This will give you a better balance and perspective when you develop your own social media posts.

- Develop a daily and weekly schedule. Your weekly schedule should be dedicated to time given to writing and publishing your practice's blog articles. Some people prefer to write a week or month's worth of blog posts all at once, and publish them over time. Others prefer to write and publish an article at a time, on a daily or weekly basis. Your daily schedule should carve out time to monitor what others are saying in your social media networks, as well as to post and monitor your own posts at least once or twice each day. This requires discipline, as it is easy to fall prey to the lure of monitoring social media several times a day, or even hourly. Don't fall into this time-killing pattern! Rely on your alerts and limit the time you actually go to sites, to once or twice each day. This should take no more than ten minutes per visit.

- Use a smartphone that is capable of running social media applications. This will save you an incredible amount of time and allow you to monitor your networks more frequently without taking too much time away from your other duties. It also enables you to post photographs and video within seconds of taking them without having to sit at a computer, download your images, and then upload them to your site.

- Create a "library" of material by looking for books of quotations or "fun facts" that have animal sections. Another great source for compiling a resource library is to use another social media network called Stumble Upon (http://www.stumbleupon.com) to find online images and blog posts that are specific to pets. This site asks you to build a profile, based on your interests. Then as you use the "stumble" button, it finds sites of interest for you. You can then choose to "favorite" a site or photo and save it for future use as you develop your social media posts. Set aside a small amount of time each week to "stumble" and build your resource pool.

- Give your team members digital cameras and ask them to take photos for you. You can either have them email the photos to you, or you can download the images once a day and use them throughout the week.

- Ask your veterinarians and team members to write blog posts for you. If everyone took the time to write one article, on a topic that interested them, you would have several weeks of blog posts ready and waiting to be edited and published.

- Pay attention to your weekly statistics and reports from each social media platform you use, including your blog site statistics. This will keep you on track, developing posts around topics that have garnered the most activity and limiting those that receive little or no interest.

- Gradually train another team member to "speak with the practice's voice". You can then give them administrative access to your social media networks, so you have someone else who can create posts and respond to comments and questions. On Twitter, you would simply give them your user name and password. On Facebook, you can assign any number of people who follow your business page administrative access, by selecting the "make admin" button next to their name when you "view all" people who "like" your practice's page.

Create a weekly routine that works for you and stick to it. This takes discipline, but is well worth it when your other duties don't suffer.

Social Media and Mobility

If we look at Asia today as a forecast for the future of technology in the United States, we can only look forward to increased mobility each year. The rise of the Smartphone, along with the applications that turn these phones into miniature, portable computers have revolutionized the way we connect with one another and with the Internet. Clients no longer need to sit down at their desktop to connect with the web. They simply use their phone from wherever they happen to be at any given moment.

What does this mean for your practice? It's even more important that you master these new ways of connecting and bonding with your clients, as things will be changing dramatically in a very short time. You need to keep up with technology, rather than wait for it to take on its "final format", as this will probably never happen. Social media and technology is changing so quickly that by the time you decide to join in, you'll be behind the curve.

If we take a look at some of the things that are happening in other professions and industries in 2010, we may be able to gauge what to prepare for in our very near future:

- Text message reminders

- Text message appointment reminders and confirmations

- Text message post-op and hospitalization updates

- Pet portals applications for Smartphones

- Smartphone applications customized to your veterinary practice

- Online veterinary pharmacy Smartphone applications

If we take a look at the present, there are several opportunities already available to make your practice's presence more mobile:

- Foursquare, Gowalla, Facebook places, Yelp and other Smartphone applications that focuses on geographic location and "check-ins" are definitely at the top of your mobility tool list. There's no clear winner in this venue yet, as users seem to be hopping around from one to the other. It appears that users want to use the application where most of their other friends can be found. Several of these applications can be linked to both Facebook and Twitter, broadcasting "check-ins" across multiple platforms at once. The power behind these tools rests in the underlying endorsement that occurs when clients "check-in" at your practice. They are essentially broadcasting their presence at your specific veterinary practice. You can sponsor "check-in" deals on each site, encouraging clients to "check-in", such as free or discounted nail trims, or a coupon towards their pet food purchase.

- Facebook and Twitter have Smartphone applications that are seeing a tremendous increase of use. More and more social media users are relying on these Smartphone applications to keep them abreast of what's happening with their friends, no matter where they are or what they are doing. Taking a photo with a Smartphone, then posting it to your social media network, along with a status update takes less than five seconds with these mobile applications.

- Heartgard Plus (by Merial) has a free Smartphone application that enables clients to store their pets' information and receive monthly push notifications to remind them to administer their pet's heartworm prevention. This app enables a client to store your practice's contact information in their pet's file, creating a one-touch connection to you should they have questions or need to schedule an appointment. It also reminds clients when they are running low on Heartgard Plus, and reminds them to purchase more, compliance dream-come-true!

- Veterinary-specific apps are on the rise to aid you and your team in providing on-the-spot answers. From dog and cat first aid, to Webster's DIA, or a great little app called A Vet Tool that has everything from a full cat and dog formulary to fluid rate, gestation, and dosage calculators. These apps offer veterinary professionals mobility at an affordable rate.

While you might not find the *perfect* Smartphone application yet, what you should be thinking about is the potential for the future. By embracing mobility now, you will start thinking about the future and pointing your practice in the right direction for growth.

Social Media Policy: Creating Your Practice's Guidelines and Protocols

As with any policy or protocol you have in your hospital, unless it's written down, it doesn't really exist. Unless you operate as a "one-man-show", you need to create a written social media policy for your practice so that everyone understands several things:

- The purpose of social media in your practice

- The platforms and networks your practice will be using

- Who is authorized to participate on behalf of the practice, and when they will be participating

- Boundaries and guidelines all team members should respect

- Steps that should be followed during a social media crisis (negative publicity or remarks within social media networks)

- Confidentiality guidelines relevant to social media posts

- Possible repercussions should team members breech confidentiality or fail to follow the policy

Now that you have opened the social media can-of-worms, the last thing you want to happen is for your entire team to think it's open season for on-the-clock Facebook time. Personal social media has no place in the workplace and this needs to be made clear to your team. Writing a policy, training your team, and leading by example can accomplish this. Practices who think they should just ban Facebook altogether and forget about social media because it's too difficult to police should think about this: if you have telephones in your practice and you are able to limit personal telephone calls, then you can do the same with social media. The key is to have policies in place and enforce them fairly.

By the same token, you may *expect* your veterinarians and key team members to participate in your social media strategy, but they may not be prepared to do so for several reasons. They may not be familiar with social media on a personal level. It is not uncommon to find team members who have heard negative things about social media take a stance against it. You will need to work closely with your team members to help them see the benefits, as well as teach them how they can successfully minimize the negative things they have heard. Just as they were trained to use the telephone and perhaps email in your practice to communicate with clients, they will also need to be trained to use social media for the same reason: to communicate with potential and existing clients.

Alternatively, you may have veterinarians and team members who have given little thought to their professional persona when participating in social media networks. They may feel uncomfortable with some of the information that can be found in their profile if a client or co-worker were to read it. Again, training and modeling professional behavior will help your team manage their social media profiles more appropriately in the future. You should work with your veterinarians and team members one-on-one to determine whether they should have a separate "professional" profile, or if they can easily "clean up" their current profile and manage things by way of privacy settings. Maintaining one profile is certainly much easier than trying to keep track of multiple profiles, as you always run the risk of mistakenly posting things to the wrong profile when trying to maintain multiple online identities. As social media has become more prevalent in the workplace, we are seeing trends of people maintaining multiple online profiles, using their real names for their "professional" identity and a pseudonym for their "close friends and family" identity. As long as separate email addresses are used, this is perfectly acceptable in most social networks.

If you have purchased this book and would like a social media policy template that can be customized to your practice, and your intent is to use it strictly for your practice, then email me at artdogindy@facebook.com with the following details:

In the subject line, type the phrase: Social Media Policy Template. Please tell me where and when you purchased your copy of this book and include your full name, practice name, and return email address. In return, I will email you a Word document attachment that you can use as a template for writing your own social media policy.

Social Media Training for Your Team

With a written social media policy and protocol in place, you are now ready to conduct your team-training program. While you might feel members of your team are better equipped to train you than the other way around when it comes to Facebook, using social media does not qualify someone to have a full understanding of the impact it can potentially have on your practice and possibly their career. The first time I conducted social media training with my staff, it was an eye-opening experience for myself, as well as the entire team.

Right now, your team probably only has experience with social media from a personal perspective. This means they have approached it as something completely separate from their work life, with little or no consideration as to how it could impact their careers. You need to enlighten them, so they have a better understanding of how to conduct themselves online, as well as how to better protect their privacy. I stated earlier that I accept "friend requests" from any and all staff members who send me an invitation to be friends on Facebook. Many friends and colleagues have asked me why I would open myself up to this? Shouldn't I draw the line with staff? My answer to this is that the only way I can model behavior to my team members is to allow them access to the way I conduct myself in this forum. This requires them to be my "friend", as I employ privacy settings to protect myself on Facebook. By modeling appropriate social media behavior, my hope is that I can prevent team members from making mistakes that can damage their careers, or the reputation of the practice.

Start your team training session by explaining what the practice is doing, in terms of social media and why. You should share with them your full social media strategy, so they understand you are marketing the practice, as well as enhancing client bonding and communication. Share some examples of practices that have done this with great success (see resources section of this book for examples). You should then distribute copies of your practice's written social media policy to everyone. As you read through the policy, list the networks you will be using and how each one works. Just because a team member is active on Facebook does not mean they have ever read a blog, or understand how Twitter works. Take time to make sure everyone understands the differences. If you can, pulling up the networks on your computer and displaying them on a projector screen will help the team work through the discussion and you'll be better equipped to answer questions. At one team training session, as I was explaining Twitter to the group, I showed a thread of conversation between @BRACpet and a client within the clinic's newsfeed. One team member raised her hand and said, "You mean you actually talk to clients and they talk back to you on Twitter?!" It was a definite "ah-ha" moment for her, as well as others.

The next point you should cover in your team-training session is who will be using social media while at work, when they will be using it, and what they are expected to be doing when visiting specified social media networks. During this discussion it should be pointed out that these key individuals have been given additional work responsibilities (not to be confused with privileges). You have not given anyone the "freedom" to use social media at work; you have placed added responsibilities on certain individuals to accomplish specific tasks, using the tools available on specific social networks. Your team needs to understand that when they see a co-worker on Facebook, they aren't "playing around"; they are performing a delegated task, as an integral part of their job. This is a great opportunity to discuss accountability. Let the entire team know that this is a "work-in-progress", and that as you try to integrate these new tasks into the daily routine, it might take more time than anticipated. If team members find their co-workers are struggling to perform their social media duties at the "right" time each day, or it seems to take them away from their other duties for longer than anticipated, they need to be able to discuss this with their peers. Give the entire team *permission* to give open, honest feedback to their peers.

Once you have worked through explaining your social media policy, you should discuss privacy settings and client-patient confidentiality with your team. Even the most experienced Facebook users are sometimes oblivious to their privacy settings. You should conduct a tutorial with your team, explaining the differences between allowing "everyone" to have access to their wall, photos, etc. and allowing only "friends" or "friends of friends" to have access to areas of their profile. If individuals leave their privacy settings open to "everyone", they are giving unrestricted access of their information to the entire Facebook community. It is usually much wiser to restrict access to "friends" only, or "friends of friends" to protect your basic privacy. In many cases, team members will have listed your practice as their employer. In doing so, this does open them up to being discoverable to clients who search Facebook using your practice's name. While there is nothing wrong with this, a few things should be taken into consideration. If a team member lists your practice name on their profile, they should understand that statements made by them could be interpreted as the opinion of the practice, when this might not necessarily be true. This is a very valid example for the needed use of privacy settings and controls. Furthermore, broadcasting negative statements about the practice or their supervisors in a social media network could jeopardize their employment with your practice.

More important than privacy settings and friend requests, client and patient confidentiality needs to be addressed in your social media staff training. The very nature of social media leads to interpersonal interactions that could potentially cross the lines of patient and client confidentiality. You must do your best to protect the confidentiality of your clients and their pets at all times. There are a few different ways of handling this.

- You can choose to never mention clients or patients by name. You can discuss cases in the social media forum by changing names to protect the identities of your clients and their pets. You can also post digital x-rays and photos you have taken of pets without using their real names.

- You can ask clients if they would grant permission to use their images and/or names in your social media posts. Many clients enjoy having their stories told and are more than happy to give you their permission. You should document the level of permission granted, and keep it on file. You can do this on a case-by-case basis, or keep a blanket statement of permission that you renew each year.

- Keep in mind that clients choose their own online identities. They may be fictitious, they may use a nickname, or they may go by their given name. Whatever identity they choose to use, you are safe to respond to their questions within the social media venue, as they have control over their own identity, level of confidentiality and privacy.

You need to take the time to explain the methods you'll be using, during your staff training. Giving team members real life examples will help with their understanding of this complex issue. While it may be perfectly fine with clients to interact with one another, posting comments and questions, team members need to remember they are still employees of the practice when they interact in this venue. They have to pay more attention to what they are saying than the average person, as your clients know them as members of your staff and it is implied that what they say or post is within the context of your practice's communications.

Example:

You post a radiograph of a dog's abdomen on your Facebook page. The x-ray image is very interesting, as several baby pacifiers can be seen in the stomach. You post the question, "How many pacifiers can you see?" with the digital photo and wait to see what interest evolves. Over the course of the next hour, a dozen clients guess the number of pacifiers and make comments that they hope the dog is doing well. You make a comment that the dog is doing just fine along with a photo showing the total number of pacifiers that were found in the dog's stomach. A staff member makes a comment after this photo, stating: "Rufus is doing really well. We love the Carters! We'll see you soon to visit Rufus☺" This is an example of a breach of confidentiality. Even though your staff member had nothing but the best of intentions, she revealed your patient and client's names, along with the patient's condition. A more appropriate way to post to this thread, while maintaining confidentiality would have been:

"Dr. Jones performed surgery and all is well with this pup!" Asking a team member to remove a comment, when they make an error is the best course of action. You should also discuss the reason for your request along with the wording for a more appropriate replacement post.

Not only do you need to respect the confidentiality of your clients and patients, but also you must give consideration to the privacy of your team members. As part of your practice's social media strategy to bond your existing clients to your practice, you may decide to post photos and information about members of your staff: birthdays, anniversaries, continuing education news, etc. You should create a statement of release, allowing your team to choose their individual levels of participation. Offer them the options to:

- Use their image only

- Use their image and first name only

- Use their image and full name

- Opt out of your practice's social media strategy (no images or names)

You will probably encounter few, if any who opt out. Most team members are comfortable allowing the use of their image and first name, if not their image and full name. Keep this release on file, once completed and signed, in each employee's personnel record.

As your practice begins to implement your social media strategy, be sure to share examples, and success stories with your team on a frequent basis. As everyone becomes more and more familiar with social media, the more they'll be able to contribute by taking photos and coming up with new ideas.

Social media is not something you can do overnight. You can't read this book, set everything up, work on it a few weeks and expect big changes overnight. You need to work at social media. You need to nurture it and participate in the forum. If you think of it with the fable of the tortoise and the hare in mind, you want to be the tortoise when it comes to social media. The veterinarians and practices that do a little bit each day, over a long period of time will be surprised at the progress they have made after a year. The first year may be slow, but the second year will more than likely show real return on your investment in time and energy. Build your brand, attract your community, and then manage your reputation through transparency, trust and professionalism with an added dash of your true personality.

Glossary of Social Media Terms and Abbreviations

@: This symbol is used to signify someone's Twitter handle (@BRACpet, @AAHAHelpingPets, @IndyHumane). It is also used to "tag" individuals in Facebook posts, as well as to speak directly to someone in a thread of comments.

#: This symbol is a hashtag. It is used to pull information into searchable streams of information. A hashtag in front of a word makes it a searchable post (#Indy, #veterinary). If you want to make a phrase searchable, then you put a hashtag in front of it, and eliminate all spacing in the phrase (#catsanddogs, #petinsurance, #woofwednesday, #meowmonday, #followfriday, #pawsforpeace)

#followfriday: A common practice found on Twitter on Fridays each week. Twitter users will recommend to others someone they should follow, along with a brief reason for following them, followed by #followfriday.

#meowmonday: A common phrase used on Twitter on Mondays to signify topics relevant to cats, cat lovers, or anything to do with cats.

#woofwednesday: A common phrase used on Twitter on Wednesdays to signify topics relevant to dogs, dog lovers, or anything to do with dogs.

Blog: online journal; web + log

Comment: on Facebook, when a wall post is made, users have the ability to add their thoughts or respond directly to the post or question by selecting the "comment" button, which opens a box into which they can type their thoughts, creating a thread of related posts.

Community: group of like-minded individuals who follow or like the same celebrity, business, organization, or cause in a social media network, participating and interacting with the primary user or administrator, as well as with one another.

DM: This is an abbreviation for "direct message" on Twitter. In order to DM another user, you must follow them and they must follow you in return. A "DM" cannot be seen by other users; it is a private message sent between two users on Twitter.

E-newsletter: electronic newsletter that is delivered through electronic mail.

Follow: To follow someone, either on Twitter or Facebook, means to pull their posts into your news feed and make them a part of your personal social media community.

Follower: denotes someone who subscribes to your social media posts.

Friend: on Facebook, a friend is someone with whom you have an established online relationship by way of approving an invitation.

Friend request: on Facebook, to send an invitation to become friends.

Like: on Facebook, this button is found on business and celebrity pages. When a Facebook user presses the "like" button on a page, they pull that page's wall posts into their personal news feed. "Like" is also an option found on most Facebook posts that allows user to simply express their agreement with a particular post without commenting further.

News feed: your personalized feed of posts from others you choose to follow or friend in social media networks. Social media venues are designed to pull the latest posts from those in your community into a single page for ease of viewing, in a chronological manner.

Mention: On Twitter, this means you name another user by their Twitter handle within a post. Twitter provides users with a tab labeled "mentions" making it easy to find out who is talking about you on Twitter.

Pet portal: a website that allows clients private access to their pet's medical information. A pet portal extracts data from your veterinary practice management software to keep a client's pet portal up-to-date, usually on a nightly basis.

Push notifications: certain mobile applications function by pushing text messages directly from the app to the cell phone screen, as a reminder or notification. Users have the ability to accept or decline push notifications.

RT: is an abbreviation for "retweet" on Twitter. When you post an RT, you are reposting someone else's tweet and giving them credit for the original post. The proper way to retweet is to start with RT, followed by the original user's handle, followed by their tweet. You can add to the RT, either at the beginning or end of the RT.

Thread: on Facebook, a wall post followed by multiple comments made to the original post, or to one another. On Twitter, a thread is usually a series of tweets between two users, speaking directly to one another, usually through use of the "reply" button.

Tweet: on Twitter, a typed post of 140 characters or less. A tweet can contain a link to a blog post, or online article, or other information.

Unfollow: on Twitter, a user can choose to remove another user from their newsfeed by no longer following their tweets.

Unfriend: on Facebook, a user can choose to no longer be Facebook friends with another user. This removes the other user's posts from your news feed and prevents them from having access to your wall, etc. When you "unfriend" another user, they do NOT receive notification that you have done this, but they will eventually realize it when they can no longer access your Wall.

Wall post: on Facebook, any comments, photos, links, or videos that are made directly to a page's wall.

Resources

<u>Veterinary Professionals to Follow on Twitter</u>

There are literally thousands of veterinary professionals active on Twitter. I apologize in advance if you are not listed here, but I had to edit the list down to a reasonable size. I've tried to include an eclectic mix of veterinarians, veterinary practices, industry professionals, practice managers, and pet bloggers. Choose a few to follow and interact with to get started. Get to know them, then follow others you meet when you choose to participate in this forum of tweeting and re-tweeting!

AAHA Helping Pets (Tamara Fox)	@AAHAHelpingPets
Animal Care Center of Huntington Beach	@VetLovingPetsHB
ASPCA	@ASPCA
AVMA	@AVMAvets
Bark Tutor School for Dogs	@BarkTutor
Phillip Barnes, creator of @AmandaBrownDVM	@phillipbarnes
Dr. Marty Becker	@DrMartyBecker

Berkley Animal Clinic	@BerkleyAnimal
Laura Bennett, CEO of Embrace Pet Insurance	@laurabennett
Blogpaws Team	@blogpaws
Jason Canapp, veterinary business advisor	@canapp
Community Pet Hospital	@CPHVets
Countryside Veterinary Hospital	@CountrysideVH
Cuyahoga Falls Veterinary Clinic	@fallsvetclinic
Tom Dock, certified veterinary journalist	@VetNewsNetwork
The Drake Center for Veterinary Care	@drakecentervet
dvm360.com	@dvm360
Elizabeth L. Elliott	@Animallawinfo
Embrace Pet Insurance	@EmbracePetIns
FIDO Friendly Magazine	@FIDOFriendly
Michelle Guercio, CVT, CVPM	@mguercio
Halo Purely for Pets	@halopets
Roxanne Hawn, award-winning dog blogger	@roxannehawn
Dr. Jim Humphries	@PetDocsOnCall
Dr. Shawn Finch	@Finch93
Firstline Magazine	@FirstlineMag
Paul Fisher, CVPM	@Triathalon_Dude
Dr. Brian C. Hurley	@drbhurley

Shelley Johnson, CVPM	@Co42CVPM
Dr. Nancy Kay	@speakingforspot
Dr. Patty Khuly	@dolittler
Dr. Jennifer Koehl	@VMDiva
Mandi Martinez, practice manager	@rahmandi
Jason Merrihew, AAHA	@HealthyPet
Jim Nash, CVPM	@jim_nash
NAVC	@The_NAVC
NAVTA	@VetTechs
Dr. Kristin Nelson	@DrKristenNelson
Newport Beach veterinary Hospital	@NewportVet
NorthStar VETS	@NorthStarVETS
Olathe Animal Hospital	@oaholathe
Pet Connection Team	@petconnection
Dr. Joann Righetti	@JoanneRighetti
Jason Scott's cat	@Sockington
Dr. Janet Tobiassen	@AboutVetMed
Trupanion Pet Insurance (Stacy)	@Trupanion
Dr. Geoff Tucker	@EquinePractice
Valley Cottage Animal Hospital	@VCAH

Veterinary Hospital Managers Association	@VHMAssoc
Vet Partners	@VetPartners
Veterinary Pet Insurance	@VPI
Vet-Stem	@VetStem
Dr. Ernie Ward	@drernieward
Wedgewood Pharmacy	@WedgewoodPetRx
Wiley-Blackwell	@VetUpdates
Dr. Sophia Yin	@SophiaYin
Dr. Erin Zaring	@IndyMobileVet

Facebook Pages From the Veterinary Community

There are literally thousands of veterinary professionals who have created Facebook pages for their veterinary practices. Again, I apologize in advance if you are not listed here, but I had to edit the list down to a reasonable size. Take a look around and learn from those who have ventured forward and found success on Facebook.

Animal Hospital of Pensacola http://www.facebook.com/pages/Animal-Hospital-of-Pensacola

Broad Ripple Animal Clinic and Wellness Center http://www.facebook.com/BRACpet

Care Animal Hospital http://www.facebook.com/careanimal

Case Veterinary Hospital http://www.facebook.com/pages/Case-Veterinary-Hospital

Circle City Veterinary Specialty and Emergency Hospital
http://www.facebook.com/pages/Circle-City-Veterinary-Specialty-and-Emergency-Hospital

Community Pet Hospital http://www.facebook.com/pages/CPH-Vets

Countryside Veterinary Hospital
http://www.facebook.com/pages/Countryside-Veterinary-Hospital

Daniel Island Animal Hospital http://www.facebook.com/danielislandvet

The Drake Center for Veterinary Care
http://www.facebook.com/pages/The-Drake-Center-for-Veterinary-Care

Frontier Veterinary Hospital http://www.facebook.com/frontiervet

NorthStar VETS http://www.facebook.com/pages/NorthStar-VETS

Oakhurst Veterinary Hospital
http://www.facebook.com/OakhurstVeterinaryHospital

Pampered Pet Health Center
http://www.facebook.com/pages/Pampered-Pet-Health-Center

Seaside Animal Care http://www.facebook.com/pages/Seaside-Animal-Care

Seven Hills Veterinary Center http://www.facebook.com/pages/Seven-Hills-Veterinary-Center

University Animal Hospital
http://www.facebook.com/UniversityAnimalHospital

Valley Cottage Animal Hospital
http://www.facebook.com/pages/Valley-Cottage-Animal-Hospital

Veterinary Specialty Hospital
http://www.facebook.com/pages/Veterinary-Specialty-Hospital

Westlake Animal Hospital http://www.facebook.com/pages/Westlake-Animal-Hospital

Recommended Social Media Book List

Get Seen: Online Video Secrets to Building Your Business by Steve Garfield

Facebook Marketing: Designing Your Next Marketing Campaign by Justin R. Levy

The New Rules of Marketing & PR by David Meerman Scott

Six Pixels of Separation by Mitch Joel

Socialnomics: How Social Media Transforms the Way We Live and Do Business by Erik Qualman

Trust Agents: Using the Web to Build Influence, Improve Reputation, and Earn Trust by Chris Brogan and Julien Smith

Twitter Power by Joel Comm

Acknowledgements

I need to take a moment to thank several people in my life who have inspired me and helped me through the process of writing this book.

To my husband, Brock who said, "I guess this Facebook thing is kind of a big deal", as we exited the theatre after seeing the Social Network. #talesfromthebrockside

To my daughter, Jesi who rolls her eyes at the thought that her Mom is on Facebook more than she is, and actually gets paid for it;)

To my mentor, boss and friend, Dr. David Brunner. You threw down the gauntlet that ultimately led to the creation of this book and told me all along the way that I could totally do it.

To the entire team at Broad Ripple Animal Clinic and Wellness Center and Bark Tutor School for Dogs, who became the guinea pigs for all my social media experiments and training protocols. You guys are truly the BEST!! Special thanks to "Bark at Brad" and @monikawithak who have embraced social media and blazed their own paths. To Melinda: one day I WILL get you on Facebook;) Thank you all for humoring me☺

To my best friends and fellow managers who challenged me, gave me new things to think about, and kept pushing me to finish what I had started. Thank you to Lisa and Debbie who always make sure I have a roommate when I'm on the road!

And to Christine, "Yoda says thanks for everything!"